GW0069140

All Things
Wise and Wonderful

British Library Cataloguing-in-Publication Data. A catalogue record for this book is available from the British Library.

Originally published by C R Gibson Company, Norwalk, Connecticut, USA. This edition published in the UK by Eagle, an imprint of Inter Publishing Service (IPS) Ltd, St Nicholas House, 14 The Mount, Guildford, Surrey GU2 5HN.

Unless otherwise stated all Scripture quotations are taken from The Living Bible,copyright © 1971, used by permission of Tyndale House Publishers, Inc., Wheaton, IL. 60189.

Printed in Italy by LEGO

ISBN: 0 86347 217 6

All Things Wise and Wonderful

Paintings and Text by Laura Lewis Lanier

Guildford, Surrey

How can men be wise? The only way to begin is by reverence for God. For growth in wisdom comes from obeying his laws.

Psalm 111:10

Lord, I will honour and praise your name, for you are my God; you do such wonderful things!

Isaiah 25:1

Introduction

The undeniable evidence that God is who He is – Lord of all – is seen throughout creation. As I study subjects of nature to paint, I am continually amazed with the perfect order and plan for each living thing. God has a plan for our lives, but as humans, we have the free will to choose God or reject Him.

Without God, we wander aimlessly in the spiritual aspect and then wonder why life hurts and things don't make sense. We begin to question the purpose and meaning for being here, thus creating hopelessness and emptiness. Problems arise when people start "looking' for love in all the wrong places" as a country music hit expresses it. There is only One who offers real love and wisdom for direction in life – God.

It is my greatest desire and purpose in painting as well as in writing this book that you would more deeply know God through His Son, Jesus, and know that He has already made provision for all of our needs. Often this pathway to finding true happiness in life is directly opposed to our natural mind and the rest of the world's advice – because "God's ways are not our ways and his thoughts are higher than our thoughts". You can always depend on His word to be the truth and the way to real life. Our feelings and emotions are fickle guides for direction on this journey.

God's wise and wonderful counsel has made such a difference in my life and I would like to share with

you four things that have been especially powerful and meaningful to me. Yes, I hold these truths to be evident,

BELIEVE...receive Someone wise and wonderful!

OBEY...the blessings will chase you down!

BE THANKFUL...it is the key to a happy heart!

ENDURE...God is always at work!

L.L.L.

Believe

RECEIVE SOMEONE
WISE AND WONDERFUL

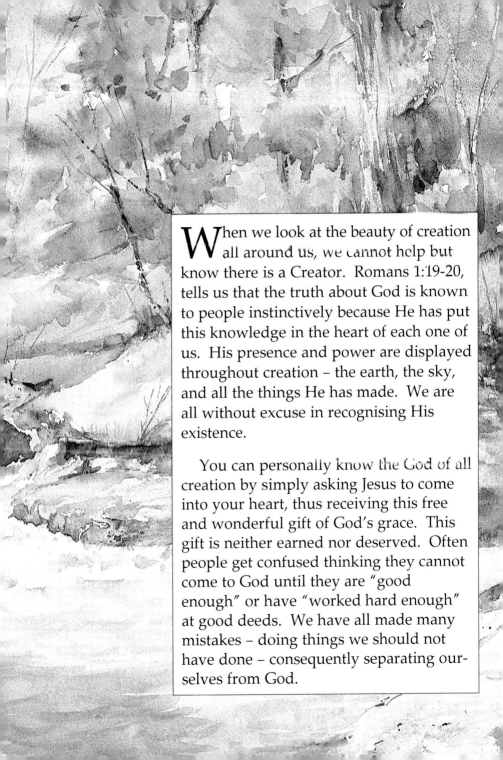

When we look at the beauty of creation all around us, we cannot help but know there is a Creator. Romans 1:19-20, tells us that the truth about God is known to people instinctively because He has put this knowledge in the heart of each one of us. His presence and power are displayed throughout creation – the earth, the sky, and all the things He has made. We are all without excuse in recognising His existence.

You can personally know the God of all creation by simply asking Jesus to come into your heart, thus receiving this free and wonderful gift of God's grace. This gift is neither earned nor deserved. Often people get confused thinking they cannot come to God until they are "good enough" or have "worked hard enough" at good deeds. We have all made many mistakes – doing things we should not have done – consequently separating ourselves from God.

But there is no way to have the debt that we owe to God paid except by receiving the payment that Jesus has made on our behalf.

God is full of love and kindness and it is His desire that all would come to know Him and enjoy His grace and peace. However God is a God of justice and He does punish sin. John 3:17–18 expresses this perfectly, "God did not send his Son into the world to condemn it, but to save it. There is no eternal doom awaiting those who trust him to save them. But those who don't trust him have already been tried and condemned for not believing in the only Son of God."

Jesus came to us as a brother to make possible a personal relationship with God our Father. When Jesus made the final payment for sin by His death on the cross, He bought for us everything we need in this life as well as eternity. Now all we have to do is believe in Him and supernaturally He makes us His very own children – caring for every need as would a loving father.

A mere intellectual knowledge of the fact that there is a God is not the meaning of the word "believe". The Greek word for believe, *pisteuo*, found in the well-known verse, John 3:16, ("For God loved the world so much that he gave his only Son, that anyone who believes in him shall not perish, but have eternal life"), means adherence to, committed to, have faith in, reliant upon, and trust in a person. It is only this surrender that produces the union and oneness with Jesus that results in salvation and eternal life.

Salvation – believing in, trusting in, and having faith in God is the first step in receiving God's true plan for your life. Hope, security, peace, joy, true happiness, and contentment are just a few of the by-products of believing in Him. God has a wonderful plan with great purpose in life for each of us – a free gift – just for the asking! Have you opened your heart to receive the only real gift that keeps on giving?

L.L.L.

*If you believe that Jesus is the Christ—that he is God's
Son and your Saviour—then you are a child of God. And
all who love the Father love his children too. So you can
find out how much you love Gods children—your brothers
and sisters in the Lord—by how much you love and obey
God. Loving God means doing what he tells us to do, and
really that isn't hard at all; for every child of God can obey
him, defeating sin and evil pleasure by trusting Christ to
help him. But who could possibly fight and win this battle
except by believing that Jesus is truly the Son of God?*

1 John 5:1-5

*Let be and be still, and know (recognise and understand)
that I am God.*

Psalm 46:10
The Amplified Bible

*Praise the Lord! For all who fear God and trust in him
are blessed beyond expression. Yes, happy is the man who
delights in doing his commands.*

Psalm 112:1

Do you want more and more of God's kindness and peace? Then learn to know him better and better. For as you know him better, he will give you, through his great power, everything you need for living a truly good life. He even shares his own glory and his own goodness with us. And by that same mighty power he has given us all the other rich and wonderful blessings he promised: for instance, the promise to save us from the lust and rottenness all around us, and to give us his own character.

But to obtain these gifts, you need more than faith; you must also work hard to be good, and even that is not enough. For then you must learn to know God better and discover what he wants you to do. Next, learn to put aside your own desires so that you will become patient and godly, gladly letting God have his way with you. This will make possible the next step, which is for you to enjoy other people and to like them, and finally you will grow to love them deeply. The more you go on in this way, the more you will grow strong spiritually and become fruitful and useful to our Lord Jesus Christ.

2 Peter 1:2-8

Jesus answered, "I am the way and the truth and the life. No-one comes to the Father except through me."

John 14:6 NIV

Jesus said to him, "Everything is possible for him who believes."

Mark 9:23 NIV

For God so greatly loved and dearly prized the world that he [even] gave up his only begotten (unique) Son, so that whoever believes in (trusts in, clings to, relies on) him shall not perish (come to destruction, be lost) but have (everlasting) life.

John 3:16
The Amplified Bible

Believe on the Lord Jesus and you will be saved.

Acts 16:31

Are there still some among you who hold that "only believing" is enough? Believing in one God? Well, remember that the devils believe this too—so strongly that they tremble in terror! Dear foolish man! When will you ever learn that "believing" is useless without doing *what God wants you to? Faith that does not result in good deeds is not real faith.*

James 2:19-20

For from the very beginning God decided that those who came to him—and all along he knew who would—should become like his Son, so that his Son would be the firstborn, with many brothers. And having chosen us, he called us to come to him; and when we came, he declared us "not guilty", filled us with Christ's goodness, gave us a right standing with himself, and promised us his glory. What can we ever say to such wonderful things as these? If God is on our side, who can ever be against us? Since he did not spare even his own Son for us but gave him up for us all, won't he also surely give us everything else?

Romans 8:29–32

And what is it that God has said? That he has given us eternal life, and that this life is in his Son. So whoever has God's Son has life; whoever does not have his Son, does not have life. I have written this to you who believe in the Son of God so that you may know you have eternal life.

1 John 5:11–13

Blessed Assurance

Blessed assurance, Jesus is mine!
Oh, what a foretaste of glory divine!
Heir of salvation, purchase of God,
Born of His Spirit, washed in His blood.

Perfect submission, perfect delight,
Visions of rapture now burst on my sight:
Angels descending bring from above
Echoes of mercy, whispers of love.

Perfect submission, all is at rest,
I and my Saviour am happy and blest:
Watching and waiting, looking above,
Filled with His goodness, lost in His love.

This is my story, this is my song,
Praising my Saviour all the day long;
This is my story this is my song,
Praising my Saviour all the day long.

Fanny Crosby

Dear Lord

*Help me to see that believing in You is so much more than
just believing that You exist. Make Yourself real to me so
that I can totally trust in, rely on, and cling to You
for everything. I want to depend on You and place my
confidence in You in order to have real life.*

*Give me the wisdom to see clearly and really understand
who Christ is and all that He has done for me. Help me to
see how incredibly great is His power to help those who
believe.*

*Forgive me when I try to run my own life instead of
allowing You to be my guide. I thank You that You have
given to believers not only the promise of eternal life and
heaven, but also the promise to take care of each day's
needs. Live in me so that I may enjoy this unique plan
You have made especially for my life. Amen.*

L.L.L.

Obey

THE BLESSINGS WILL CHASE YOU DOWN

A grand symphony with its bursting brass and smooth violins has always delighted my heart. My love for music began as a child taking piano lessons. My passion was nurtured in junior and senior high school when I learned to play the flute.

As glorious as a symphony in its entirety may sound, when its sections are broken down into separate parts and played alone, many of them make little or no sense. When singled out, cymbals are a loud crash rather than an exciting exclamation at the proper time; harmonies make a senseless sound with no real purpose or intent; and the rolling of a timpani can be as disturbing as thunder. My own lovely flute obbligatos sound like short blips of half-witted chatter.

However, as the conductor raises his arms and signals for the entire composition to be played, it is the integral parts and harmonies that create the right sound, making the melody so very beautiful and complete. Life, too, is a symphony. The conductor must be obeyed – otherwise the individual parts become ugly fragments with no real purpose or meaning.

A violinist who chooses to play whatever he pleases rather than to play the score is useless to an orchestra. And so are our lives useless if we do not follow our conductor – God. Our natural human inclination is to relate to our own intellect, emotions, or reasoning rather than trust the whole of God's plan for us which we may not see. The true pathway to a successful, blessed life depends on an uncompromising obedience to God.

L.L.L.

We can see and understand only a little about God now, as if we were peering at his reflection in a poor mirror; but someday we are going to see him in his completeness, face to face. Now all that I know is hazy and blurred, but then I will see everything clearly, just as clearly as God sees into my heart right now.

1 Corinthians 13:12

Dear brothers, don't ever forget that it is best to listen much, speak little, and not become angry; for anger doesn't make us good, as God demands that we must be.

So get rid of all that is wrong in your life, both inside and outside, and humbly be glad for the wonderful message we have received, for it is able to save our souls as it takes hold of our hearts.

And remember, it is a message to obey, not just to listen to. So don't fool yourselves. For if a person just listens and doesn't obey, he is like a man looking at his face in a mirror. As soon as he walks away, he can't see himself anymore or remember what he looks like. But if anyone keeps looking steadily into God's law for free men, he will not only remember it but he will do what it says, and God will greatly bless him in everything he does.

James 1:19–25

Don't you realize that you can choose your own master? You can choose sin (with death) or else obedience (with acquittal). For the wages of sin is death, but the free gift of God is eternal life through Jesus Christ our Lord.

Romans 6:16–23

"If you love me, obey me; and I will ask the Father and he will give you another Comforter, and he will never leave you. He is the Holy Spirit, the Spirit who leads into all truth. The world at large cannot receive him, for it isn't looking for him and doesn't recognise him. But you do, for he lives with you now and someday shall be in you. No, I will not abandon you or leave you as orphans—I will come to you. In just a little while I will be gone from the world, but I will still be present with you. For I will live again— and you will too. When I come back to life again, you will know that I am in my Father, and you in me, and I in you. The one who obeys me is the one who loves me; ... and I will reveal myself to him."

John 14:15–21

Take care to live in me, and let me live in you. For a branch can't produce fruit when severed from the vine. Nor can you be fruitful apart from me.

John 15:4

Even though Jesus was God's Son, he had to learn from experience what it was like to obey, when obeying meant suffering. It was after he had proved himself perfect in this experience that Jesus became the giver of eternal salvation to all those who obey him.

Hebrews 5:8–9

So if you are suffering according to God's will, keep on doing what is right and trust yourself to the God who made you, for he will never fail you.

1 Peter 4:19

If you fully obey the LORD your God and carefully follow all his commands that I give you today, the LORD your God will set you high above all the nations on earth. All these blessings will come upon you and accompany you if you obey the LORD your God.

Deuteronomy 28:1–2 NIV

Whether we like it or not, we will obey the Lord our God, ... for if we obey him, everything will turn out well for us.

Jeremiah 42:6

Blessings on all who reverence and trust the Lord—on all who obey him! Their reward shall be prosperity and happiness.

Psalm 128:1–2

Help me to prefer obedience to making money! Turn me away from wanting any other plan than yours. Revive my heart towards you. Reassure me that your promises are for me, for I trust and revere you.

Psalm 119:36–38

Dear Lord

Help me to obey You at all times and at all costs, for You have said that my obedience speaks louder than anything else that I could do for You. Give me the strength to do what is right. Obeying Your Word means going against my natural feelings of unbelief, fear, unforgiveness, or anger. Help me not to make my judgements by the small part I see now, but on Your Word so the end result is pleasing to You. You know my needs better than I do. Lead me on Your path to blessings and true happiness in life. Amen.

L.L.L.

Be Thankful

IT IS THE KEY
TO A HAPPY HEART

My daughters have horses and we often see them grazing in the pasture. Sometimes they awkwardly reach their heads through a fence, straining to eat the grass on the other side. I am amused at this graphic depiction of the old cliché, "the grass is always greener on the other side of the fence".

Looking around and seeing people with circumstances or things which appear better or more desirable than our own circumstances or possessions, it is easy to get caught up in the "greener grass syndrome". Even though consciously we try not to get trapped into comparisons, we do often ask God "Why?" and "How much longer?" This can cause much discouragement, jealousy, and unhappiness.

Remember that everyone has something for which to be thankful. Begin to praise God for what you do have – the many things He has already done – rather than complaining to Him for things we are lacking. Learn to be thankful in everything – whether it appears good or bad – recognise God's provision for your needs.

In Psalm 16:11, we are told that in God's presence is fullness of joy. How do you come to be in His presence? According to Psalm 100:3, we come into His gates with thanksgiving and enter His courts with praise. Praise and thanksgiving are the keys that open the door to the presence of God. The joy and happiness found in His presence are not moved by outside circumstances of life. Only here is "the peace that passes understanding" which the rest of the world does not know.

Quite often His real purposes are not seen or understood until later. We need to praise God for who He is, not just for what He does. We also need to be thankful that He is sovereign – Lord of all – and in control no matter what happens in life. As we abide in His presence, we enjoy our own specially designed green pasture.

L.L.L.

Try to realize what this means—the Lord is God!
He made us—we are his people, the sheep of his pasture.
Go through his open gates with great thanksgiving;
enter his courts with praise. Give thanks to him and bless
his name. For the Lord is always good. He is always
loving and kind, and his faithfulness goes on and on to
each succeeding generation.

Psalm 100:3–5

The one thing I want from God, the thing I seek most of all, is the privilege of meditating in his Temple, living in his presence every day of my life, delighting in his incomparable perfections and glory. There I'll be when troubles come. He will hide me. He will set me on a high rock out of reach of all my enemies. Then I will bring him sacrifices and sing his praises with much joy.

Psalm 27:4–6

Always give thanks for everything to our God and Father in the name of our Lord Jesus Christ.

Ephesians 5:20

Stay away from the love of money; be satisfied with what you have. For God has said, "I will never, never fail you nor forsake you." That is why we can say without any doubt or fear, "The Lord is my helper and I am not afraid of anything that mere man can do to me."

Hebrews 13:5–6

... I have learned how to get along happily whether I have much or little, I know how to live on almost nothing or with everything. I have learned the secret of contentment in every situation, whether it be a full stomach or hunger, plenty or want. For I can do everything God asks me to with the help of Christ who gives me the strength and power.

Philippines 4:11–13

Say "Thank you" to the Lord for being so good, for always being so loving and kind. Has the Lord redeemed you? Then speak out! Tell others he has saved you from your enemies.

He brought the exiles back from the farthest corners of the earth. They were wandering homeless in the desert, hungry and thirsty and faint. "Lord, help!" they cried, and he did! He led them straight to safety and a place to live. Oh, that these men would praise the Lord for his loving kindness, and for all of his wonderful deeds! For he satisfies the thirsty soul and fills the hungry soul with good.

Psalm 107:1–9

How we thank you, Lord! Your mighty miracles give proof that you care.

Psalm 75:1

Warn those who are lazy or wild; comfort those who are frightened; take tender care of those who are weak; and be patient with everyone. See to it that no one pays back evil for evil, but always try to do good to each other and to everyone else. Always be joyful. Always keep on praying. Always be thankful, no matter what happens, for that is God's will for you who belong to Christ Jesus.

1 Thessalonians 5:14–18.

I bless the holy name of God with all my heart. Yes, I will bless the Lord and not forget the glorious things he does for me.

He forgives all my sins. He heals me. He ransoms me from hell. He surrounds me with loving kindness and tender mercies. He fills my life with good things! My youth is renewed like the eagle's! He gives justice to all who are treated unfairly.

Psalm 103:1–6

Praise to the Lord, the Almighty

Praise to the Lord, the Almighty, the King of creation!
O my soul, praise Him, for He is thy health and salvation!
All ye who hear, Now to His temple draw near;
Praise Him in glad adoration.

Praise to the Lord, who o'er all things so wondrously reigneth,
Shelters thee under His wings, yea, so gently sustaineth!
Hast though not seen how thy desires e're have been
Granted in what He ordaineth?

Praise to the Lord, who doth prosper thy work and defend thee;
Surely His goodness and mercy here daily attend thee.
Ponder anew what the almighty can do,
If with His love He befriend thee.

Praise to the Lord, O let all that is in me adore Him!
All that hath life and breath, come now with praises
    before Him.
Let the Amen sound from His people again,
Gladly for aye we adore Him.

Joachim Neander, 1650–1680

Dear Lord

Give me a thankful heart. Help me to see with gratitude how great is Your faithfulness to us who believe. Thank You for the good work You have begun in me – I pray that You will keep right on helping me grow in Your grace until you have finally completed it. Help me always to be thankful to You for making me fit to share all the wonderful things that belong to those who live in Your Kingdom.

What a comfort it is to know that You are involved in every circumstance of my life – whether it appears good or bad – therefore I can rejoice with praise and thanksgiving that You promise to take care of all things. Thank You for the countless blessings You bestow on me, You fill my life with peace and happiness. Amen.

L.L.L.

Endure

GOD IS ALWAYS AT WORK

Running is my favourite form of exercise. A good run makes me feel revived, ready to paint and to attend to the needs of my day. On one particular occasion, I was running in a 10 K race, feeling good, doing my best time, and making it to the 6th mile. Then, at a crucial point – being tired and fairly well spent – I came to a "mountain". At this extremely steep place on the road my lungs and legs would have much preferred to run downhill! Trudging up this incredible grade, a portion of Scripture flashed in my mind, "Run the race with endurance". Yes! Here is the answer to running up all kinds of "mountains". Endurance!

Webster defines endurance as "the ability to withstand hardship, adversity, or stress ... endure: to continue in the same state: last. 2. to remain firm under suffering or misfortune without yielding. 3. to undergo (as a hardship) without giving in". In essence, endurance is when you outlast the problem.

A race is so much like life – you're going full speed, doing all that you can do – and wham! a "mountain" problem. It is during these times that those who "keep their eyes fixed on Jesus, the Author and Finisher of our faith" endure through His power and finish the race! As you meet a time of testing or difficulty, let it prove your training.

Each of us goes through times of trial and discouragement when we are tempted to give up hope. However, if you will surrender your own desires and let God be in control of your life, He will supply all of your needs. His resources are unlimited. We can choose to endure by trusting in God, because He never gives up on us and is always working for our good to successfully bring us through any difficulty to a place of victory. God's most glorious work is usually accomplished during life's most difficult challenges.

L.L.L.

Since we are surrounded by such a great cloud of witnesses, let us throw off everything that hinders, and the sin that so easily entangles, and let us run with perseverance [endurance] the race marked out for us. Let us fix our eyes on Jesus, the author and perfector of our faith.

Hebrews 12:1–2a NIV

Is your life full of difficulties and temptations? Then be happy, for when the way is rough, your patience has a chance to grow. So let it grow and don't try to squirm out of your problems. For when your patience is finally in full bloom then you will be ready for anything, strong in character, full and complete.

If you want to know what God wants you to do, ask him, and he will gladly tell you, for he is always ready to give a generous supply of wisdom to all who ask him; he will not resent it. But when you ask him, be sure that you really expect him to tell you, for a doubtful mind will be as unsettled as a wave of the sea that is driven and tossed by the wind; and every decision you then make will be uncertain, as you turn first this way, and then that. If you don't ask with faith, don't expect the Lord to give you any solid answer.

James 1:2–8

I don't mean to say I am perfect. I haven't learned all I should even yet, but I keep working towards that day when I will finally be all that Christ saved me for and wants me to be.

No, dear brothers, I am still not all I should be but I am bringing all my energies to bear on this one thing: forgetting the past and looking forward to what lies ahead, I strain to reach the end of the race and receive the prize for which God is calling us up to heaven because of what Christ Jesus did for us.

Philippians 3:12–14

In a race everyone runs but only one person gets first prize. So run your race to win. To win the contest you must deny yourselves many things that would keep you from doing your best. An athlete goes to all this trouble just to win a ribbon or a silver cup, but we do it for a heavenly reward that never disappears. So I run straight to the goal with purpose in every step. I fight to win. I'm not just shadow-boxing or playing around. Like an athlete I punish my body, treating it roughly, training it to do what it should, not what it wants to.

1 Corinthians 9:24

God is not unjust; he will not forget your work and the love you have shown him as you have helped his people and continue to help them. We want each of you to show this same diligence to the very end, in order to make your hope sure. We do not want you to become lazy, but to imitate those who through faith and patience inherit what has been promised.

Hebrews 6:10–12 NIV

I have fought the good fight, I have finished the race, I have kept the faith. Now there is in store for me the crown of righteousness, which the Lord, the righteous Judge, will award to me on that day—and not only to me but also to all who have longed for his appearing.

2 Timothy 4:7–8 NIV

Overwhelming victory is ours through Christ who loved us enough to die for us.

Romans 8:37

*When I think of the wisdom and scope of his plan I fall
down on my knees and pray to the Father of all the great family
of God ... that out of his glorious, unlimited resources he will
give you the mighty inner strengthening of his Holy Spirit. And
I pray that Christ will be more and more at home in your hearts,
living within you as you trust in him. May your roots go down
deep into the soil of God's marvellous love; and may you be able
to feel and understand, as all God's children should, how long,
how wide, how deep, and how high his love really is; and to
experience this love for yourselves, though it is so great that you
will never see the end of it or fully know or understand it. And
so at last you will be filled up with God himself.*

Ephesians 3:14–19

Amazing Grace

Amazing grace! how sweet the sound,
That saved a wretch like me!
I once was lost, but now am found,
Was blind, but now I see.

'Twas grace that taught my heart to fear,
And grace my fears relieved;
How precious did that grace appear
The hour I first believed!

Thro' many dangers, toils and snares,
I have already come;
'Tis grace that brought me safe thus far,
And grace will lead me home.

When we've been there ten thousand years,
Bright shining as the sun,
We've no less days to sing God's praise
Then when we first begun

John Newton

Dear Lord

I thank You that You are always at work and that You will never leave me or forsake me. Help me endure hardship as a good soldier who satisfies the One who enlisted him – or as an athlete who follows the rules. Fill me with Your mighty glorious strength so that I can keep on going no matter what happens – always full of the joy of the Lord. Help me to feel and understand how long, how wide, how deep, and how high Your love really is even though I will never see the end of it or fully know or understand it. What an encouragement it is to know that my ability to endure is not in me, but in Your all-powerful hand. I will continue trusting You without wavering, because You are always faithful. Amen

L.L.L.

Designed by Bob Pantelone
Edited by Eileen D'Andrea
Type set in Book Antiqua